THE PHILLIP KEVEREN SERIES

EASY HYM[N]

— PIANO LEVEL —
ELEMENTARY
(HLSPL LEVEL 2-3)

ISBN 978-0-634-07386-1

HAL•LEONARD®
CORPORATION

7777 W. BLUEMOUND RD. P.O. BOX 13819 MILWAUKEE, WI 53213

In Australia Contact:
Hal Leonard Australia Pty. Ltd.
4 Lentara Court
Cheltenham, Victoria, 3192 Australia
Email: ausadmin@halleonard.com

Visit Hal Leonard Online at
www.halleonard.com
Visit Phillip at
www.phillipkeveren.com

PREFACE

Hymns are the bedrock of the Christian faith. These timeless songs testify to the faith of our fathers. Although musical styles are always evolving, the classic melodies and texts found in these hymns remain vital.

This collection brings together some of my favorites, arranged for the developing pianist. I hope these settings will be useful in recital, worship or private time at the piano.

Sincerely,
Phillip Keveren

BIOGRAPHY

Phillip Keveren, a multi-talented keyboard artist and composer, has composed original works in a variety of genres from piano solo to symphonic orchestra. Mr. Keveren gives frequent concerts and workshops for teachers and their students in the United States, Canada, Europe, and Asia. Mr. Keveren holds a B.M. in composition from California State University Northridge and a M.M. in composition from the University of Southern California.

CONTENTS

ALL HAIL THE POWER OF JESUS' NAME

Words by EDWARD PERRONET
Altered by JOHN RIPPON
Music by OLIVER HOLDEN
Arranged by Phillip Keveren

Triumphantly

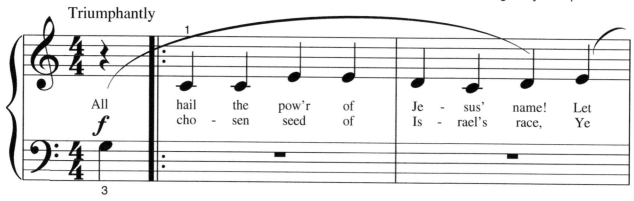

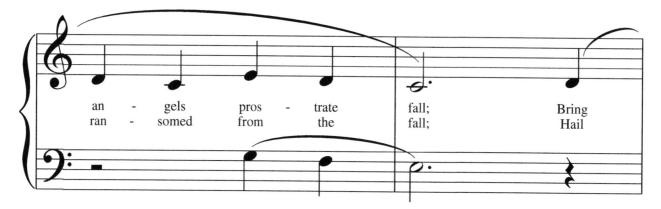

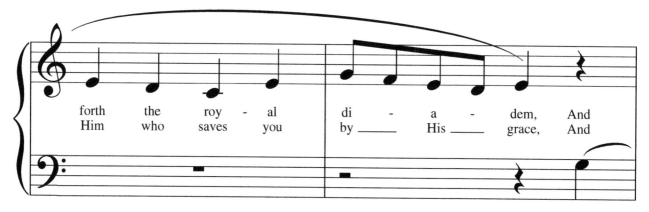

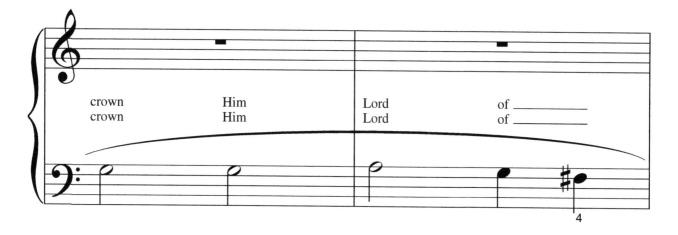

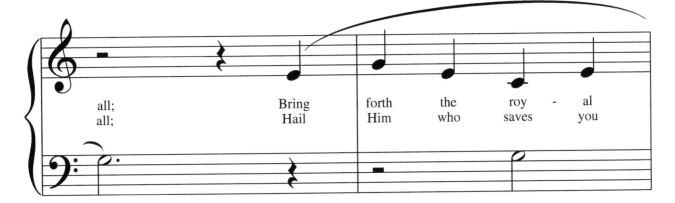

all;   Bring   forth   the   roy - al
all;   Hail   Him   who   saves   you

di - a - dem,   And   crown   Him
by _____ His _____ grace,   And   And   crown   Him

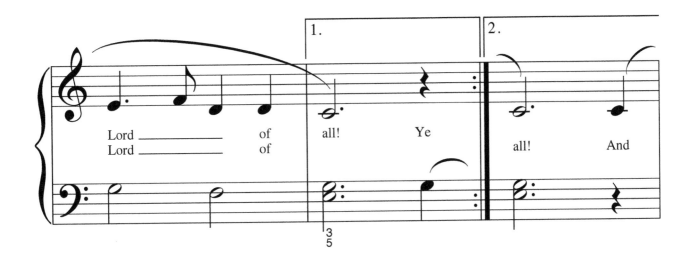

1.   2.

Lord _____ of   all!   Ye
Lord _____ of   all!   And

3
5

crown   Him   Lord _____ of   all!
rit.

3
5

BE STILL, MY SOUL

Words by KATHARINA VON SCHEGEL
Translated by KATHARINA VON SCHLEGEL
Music by JEAN SIBELIUS
Arranged by Phillip Keveren

Stately

p Be still, my soul! The

Lord is on thy side; ____

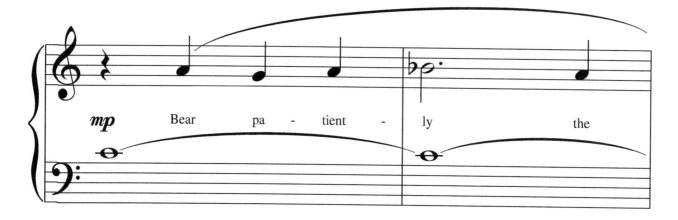

mp Bear pa - tient - ly the

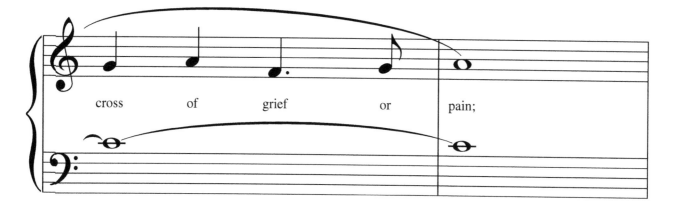

cross of grief or pain;

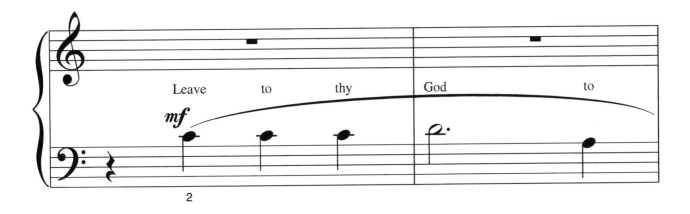

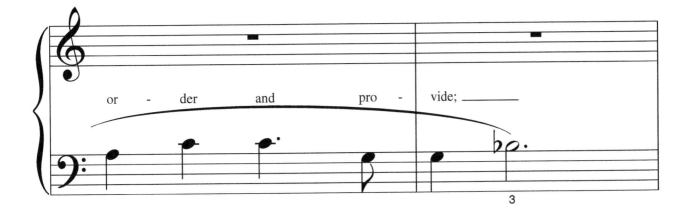

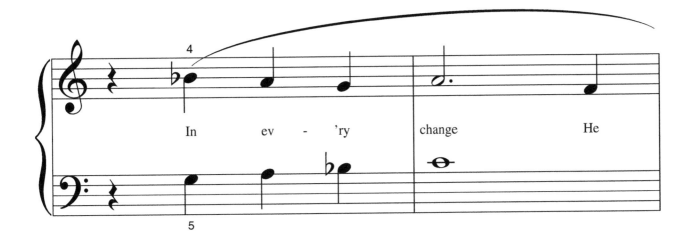

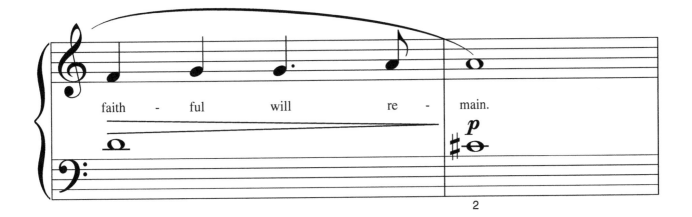

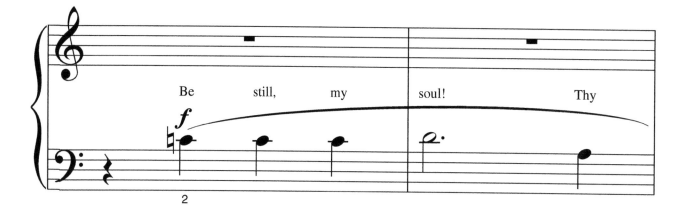

Be   still,   my   soul!   Thy

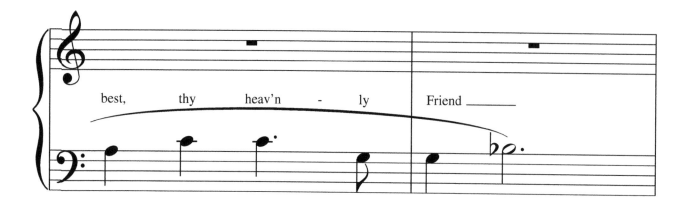

best,   thy   heav'n - ly   Friend _____

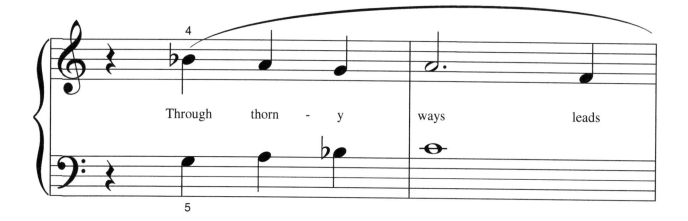

Through   thorn - y   ways   leads

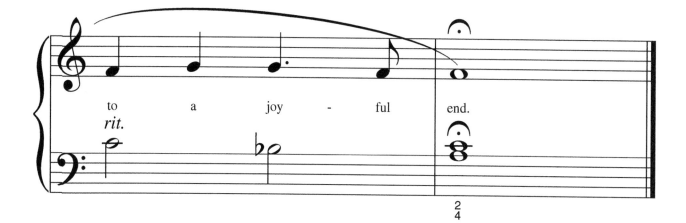

to   a   joy - ful   end.

COME, THOU LONG-EXPECTED JESUS

Words by CHARLES WESLEY
Music by ROWLAND HUGH PRICHARD
Arranged by Phillip Keveren

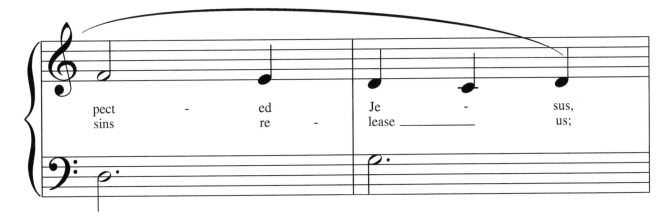

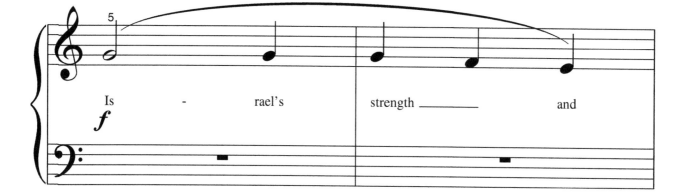

Is - rael's strength _____ and

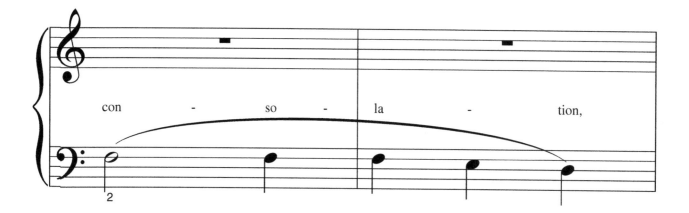

con - so - la - tion,

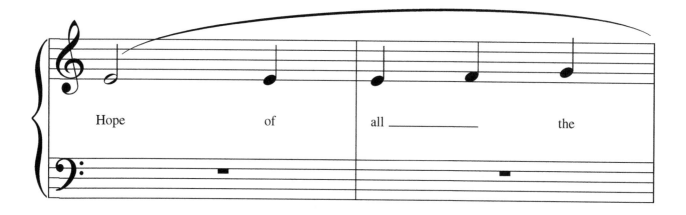

Hope of all _____ the

earth _____ Thou art;

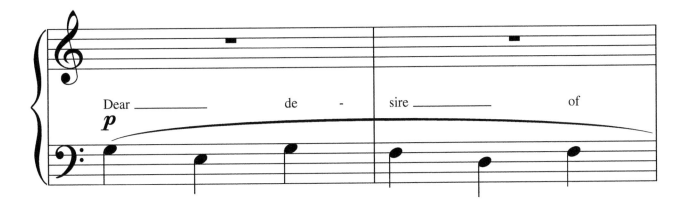

Dear _____ de - sire _____ of

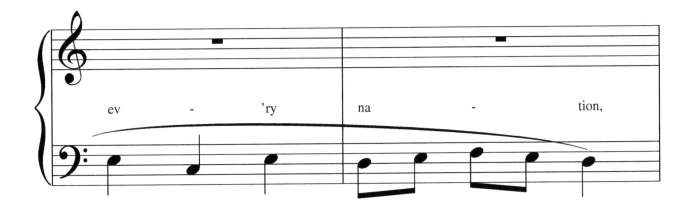

ev - 'ry na - tion,

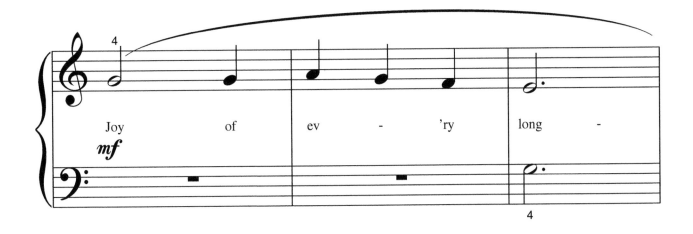

Joy of ev - 'ry long -

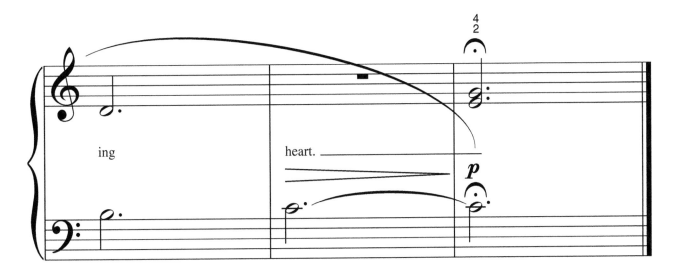

ing heart. _____

BE THOU MY VISION

Traditional Irish
Translated by MARY E. BYRNE
Arranged by Phillip Keveren

Flowing

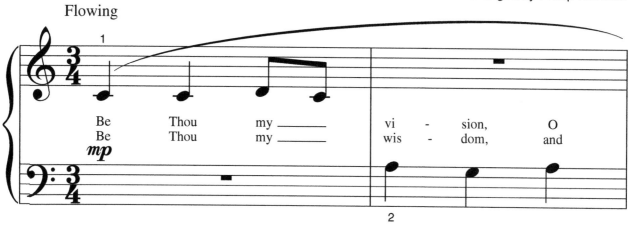

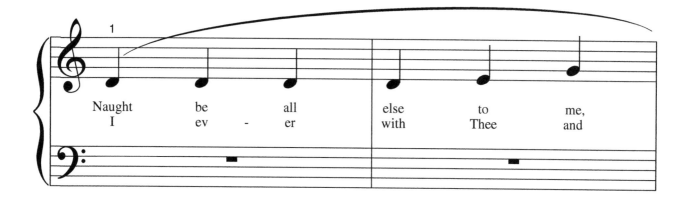

Thou my _____ best _____ thought, _____ by
Thou my _____ great _____ Fa - ther,

mf

day or by night, _____
I Thy true son, _____

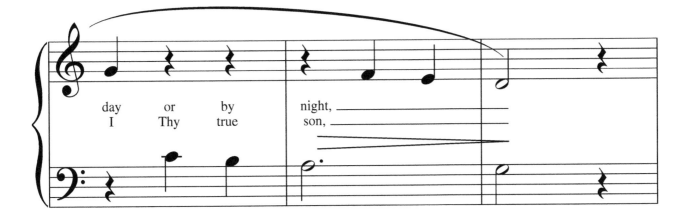

Wak - ing or sleep - ing, Thy _____
Thou in me dwell - ing, and _____

p

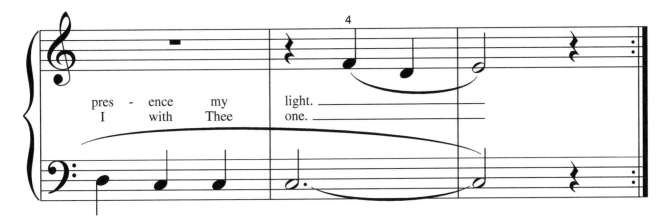

pres - ence my light. _____
I with Thee one. _____

THE CHURCH'S ONE FOUNDATION

Words by SAMUEL JOHN STONE
Music by SAMUEL SEBASTIAN WESLEY
Arranged by Phillip Keveren

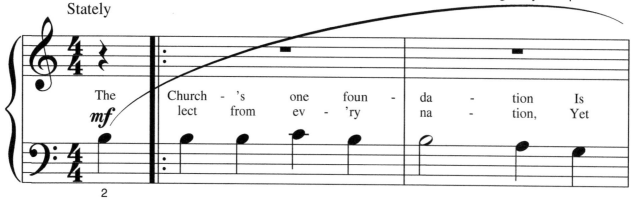

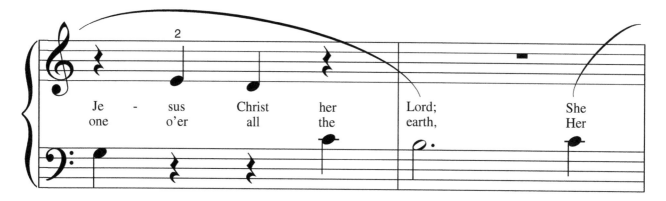

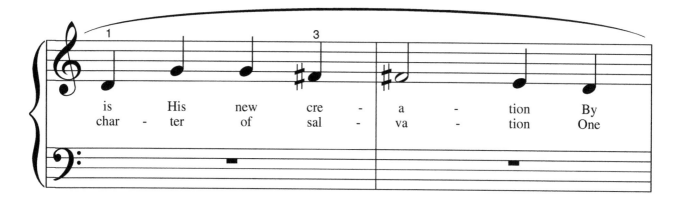

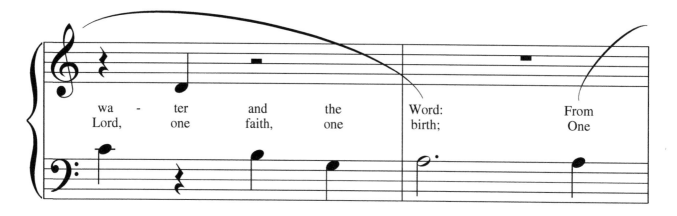

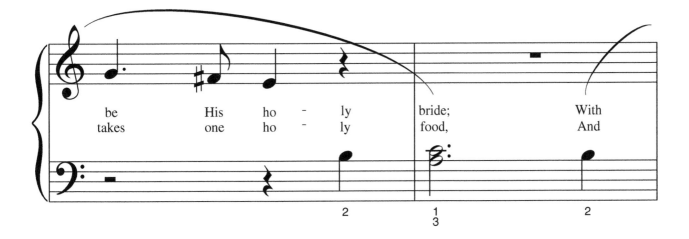

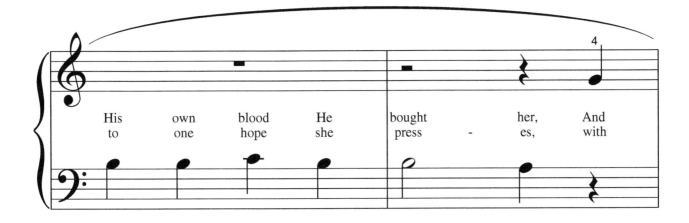

COME, THOU FOUNT OF EVERY BLESSING

Words by ROBERT ROBINSON
Music from *The Sacred Harp*
Arranged by Phillip Keveren

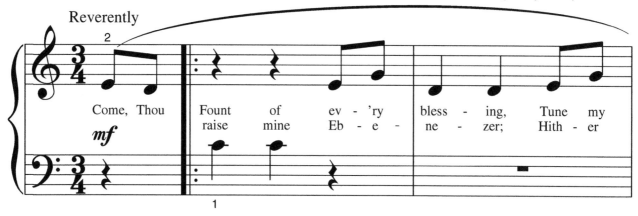

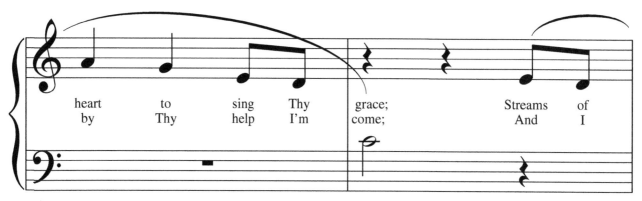

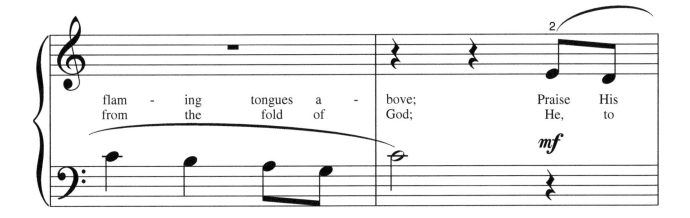

flam - ing tongues a - bove; Praise His
from the fold of God; He, to

mf

name, I'm fixed up - on it, Name of
res - cue me from dan - ger, Bought of me

God's re - deem - ing love. Here I
with His pre - cious

1.

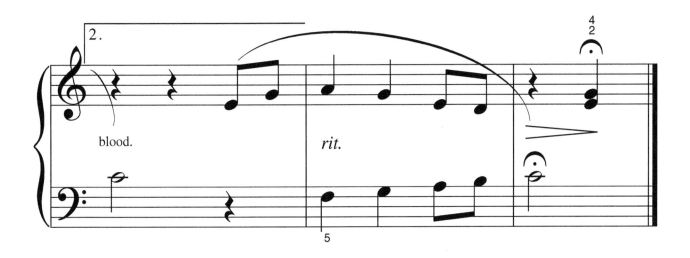

2.

blood. *rit.*

FAITH OF OUR FATHERS

Words by FREDERICK WILLIAM FABER
Music by HENRI F. HEMY and JAMES G. WALTON
Arranged by Phillip Keveren

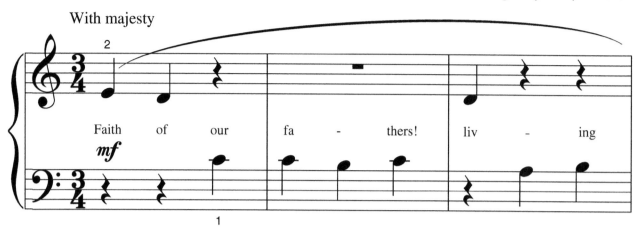

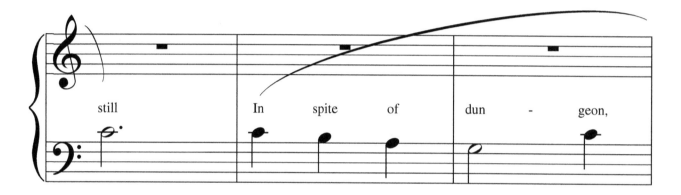

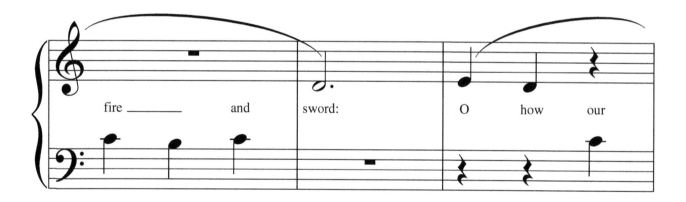

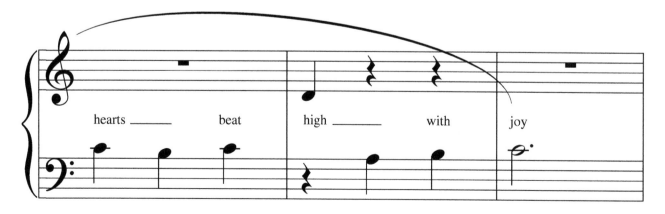

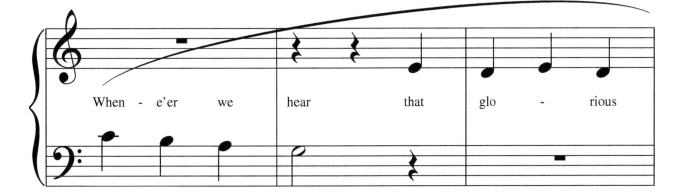

When - e'er we hear that glo - rious

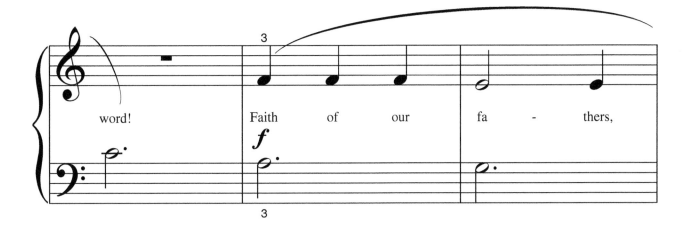

word! Faith of our fa - thers,

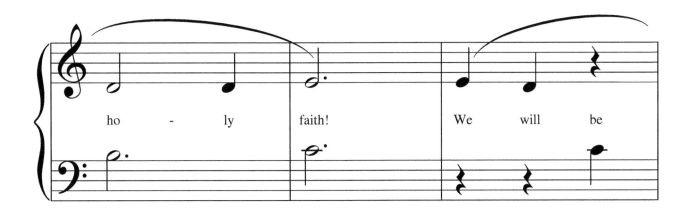

ho - ly faith! We will be

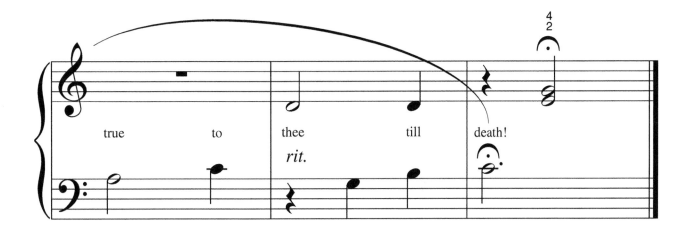

true to thee till death!

HE LEADETH ME

Words by JOSEPH H. GILMORE
Music by WILLIAM B. BRADBURY
Arranged by Phillip Keveren

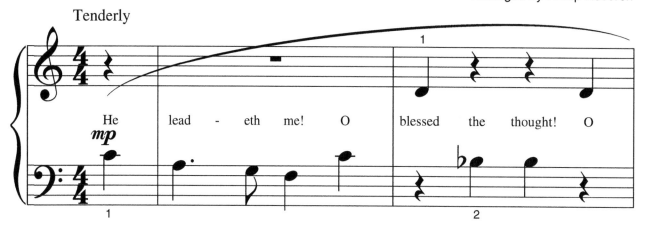

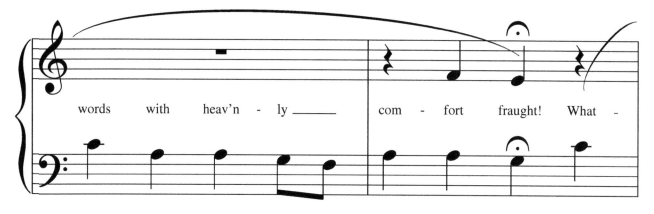

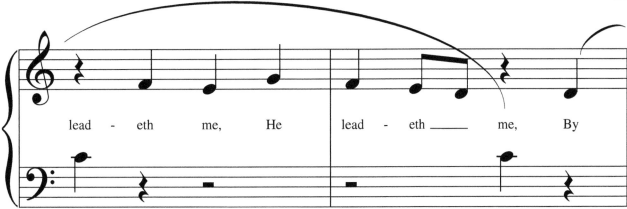

lead - eth me, He   lead - eth ____ me, By

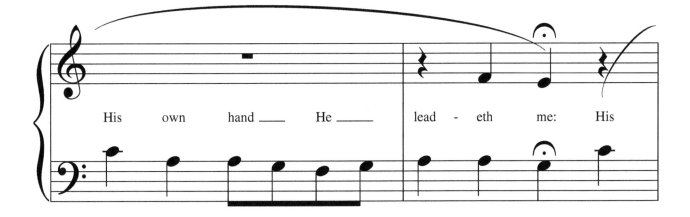

His   own   hand ____   He ____   lead - eth   me: His

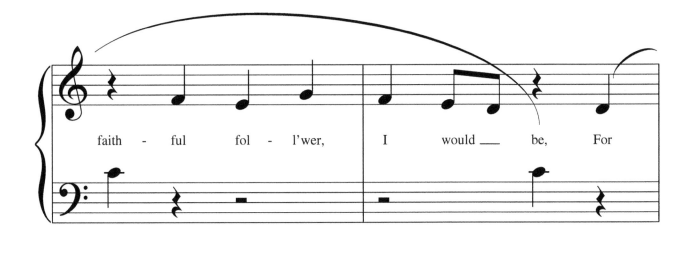

faith - ful   fol - l'wer,   I   would ____ be,   For

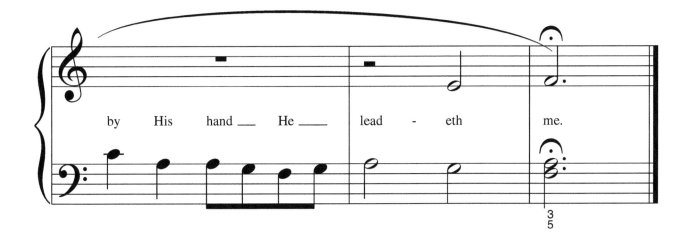

by   His   hand ____   He ____   lead - eth   me.

3
5

HOW FIRM A FOUNDATION

Traditional text compiled by JOHN RIPPON
Traditional music compiled by JOSEPH FUNK
Arranged by Phillip Keveren

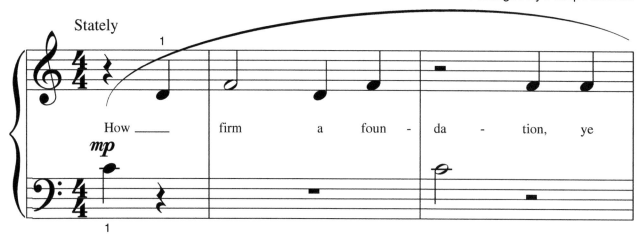

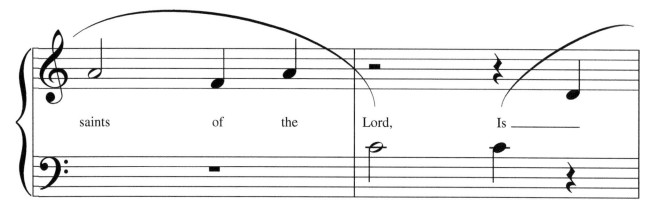

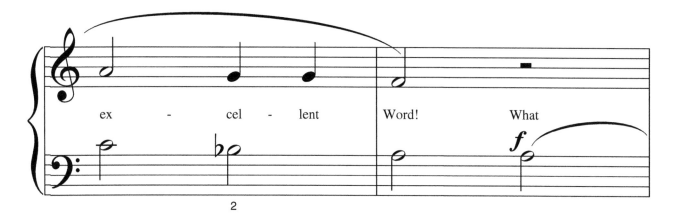

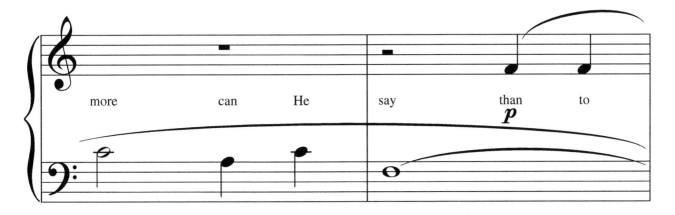

more can He say than to **p**

you He hath said, To _____ **mf**

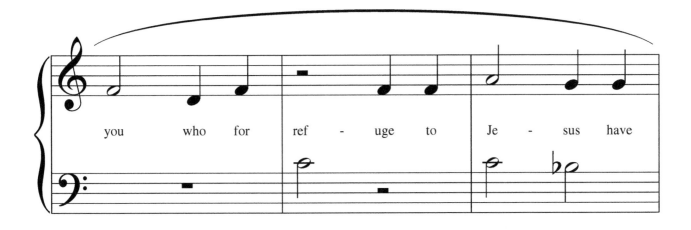

you who for ref - uge to Je - sus have

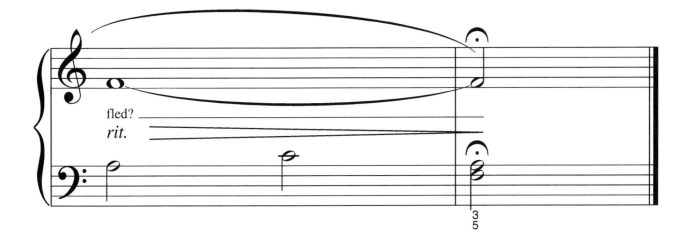

fled? _____ *rit.*

3
5

I SURRENDER ALL

Words by J.W. VAN DEVENTER
Music by W.S. WEEDEN
Arranged by Phillip Keveren

Reverently

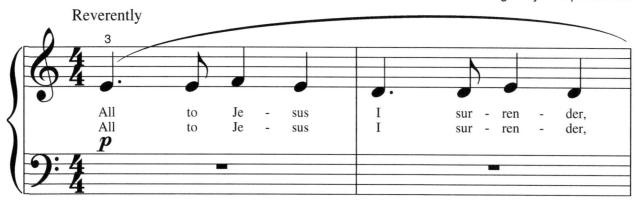

All to Je - sus I sur - ren - der,
All to Je - sus I sur - ren - der,

All to Him I free - ly give;
Hum - bly at His feet I bow;

I will ev - er love and trust Him,
World - ly pleas - ures all for - sak - en,

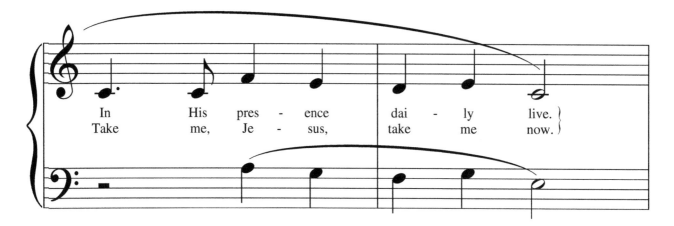

In His pres - ence dai - ly live.
Take me, Je - sus, take me now.

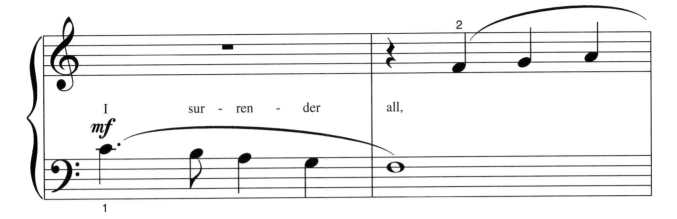

I sur - ren - der all,

I sur - ren - der all. All to Thee, my

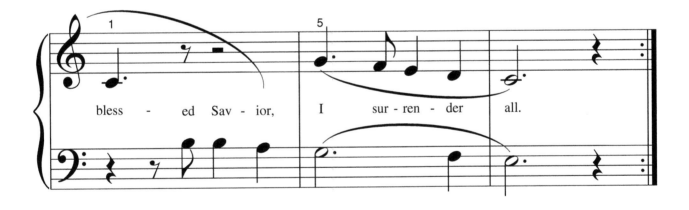

bless - ed Sav - ior, I sur - ren - der all.

I sur - ren - der all.

rit.   *p*

JOYFUL, JOYFUL, WE ADORE THEE

Words by HENRY VAN DYKE
Music by LUDWIG VAN BEETHOVEN
Adapted by EDWARD HODGES
Arranged by Phillip Keveren

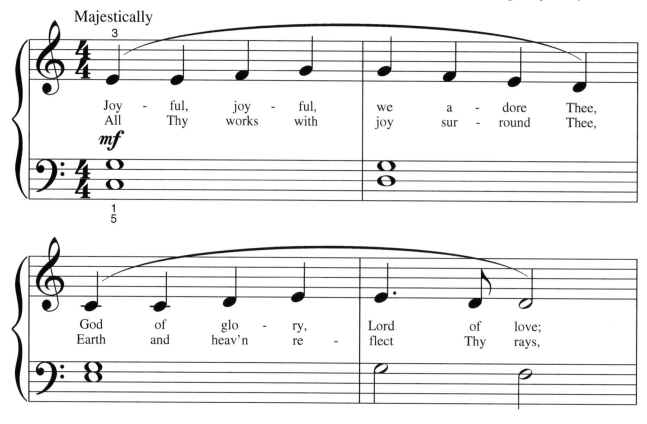

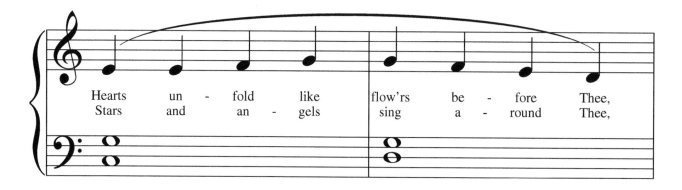

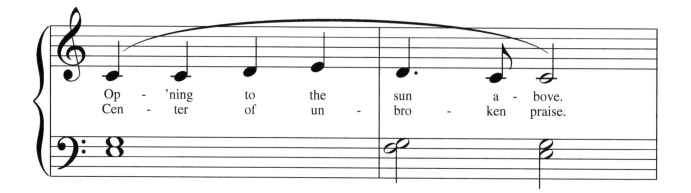

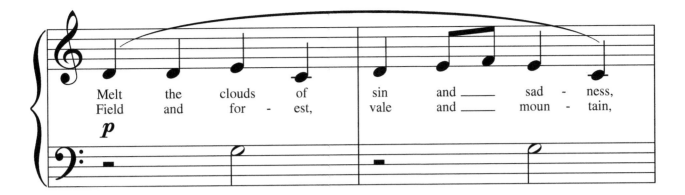

Melt the clouds of sin and ___ sad - ness,
Field and for - est, vale and ___ moun - tain,

p

Drive the ___ dark of doubt a - way;
Flow - 'ry ___ mead - ow, flash - ing sea,

cresc.

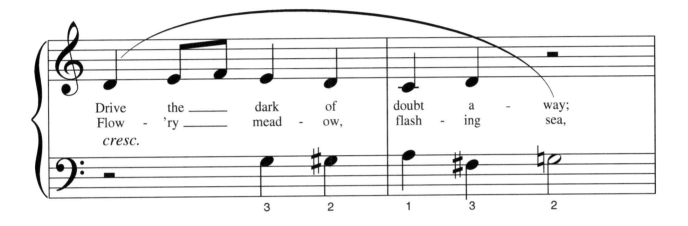

Giv - er of im - mor - tal glad - ness, Fill us with the
Chant - ing bird and flow - ing foun - tain, Call us to re -

f

light of day.
joice in Thee.

rit.

NEARER, MY GOD, TO THEE

Words by SARAH F. ADAMS
Music by LOWELL MASON
Arranged by Phillip Keveren

Serenely

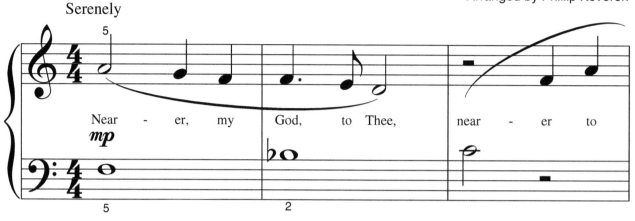

Near - er, my God, to Thee, near - er to

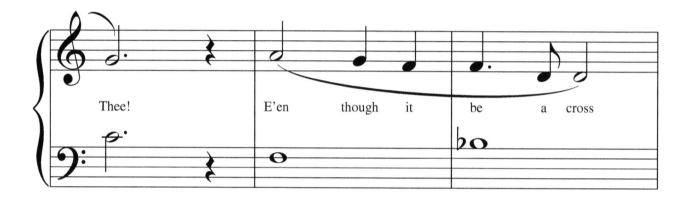

Thee! E'en though it be a cross

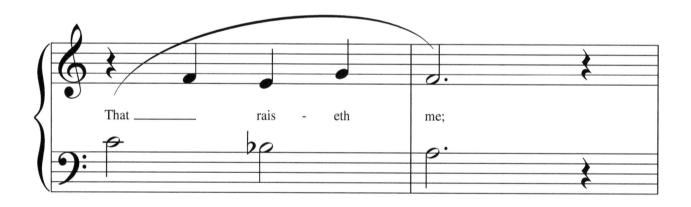

That _____ rais - eth me;

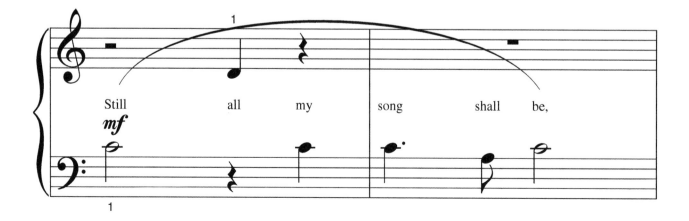

Still all my song shall be,

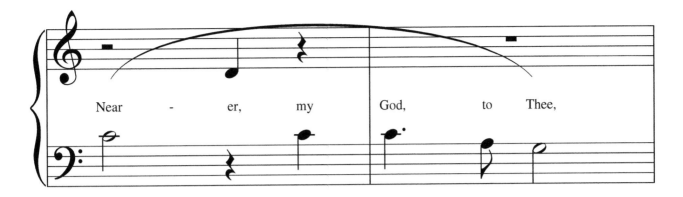

Near - er, my God, to Thee,

Near - er, my God, to Thee,

Near - er to Thee! Near -

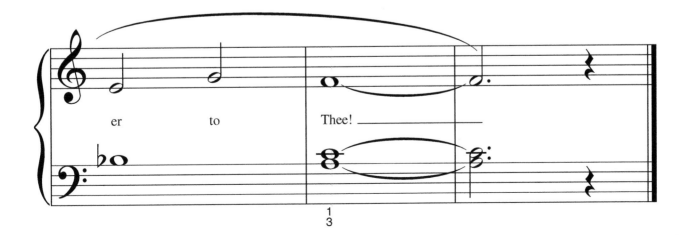

er to Thee!

PRAISE TO THE LORD, THE ALMIGHTY

Words by JOACHIM NEANDER
Translated by CATHERINE WINKWORTH
Music from *Erneuerten Gesangbuch*
Arranged by Phillip Keveren

With fanfare

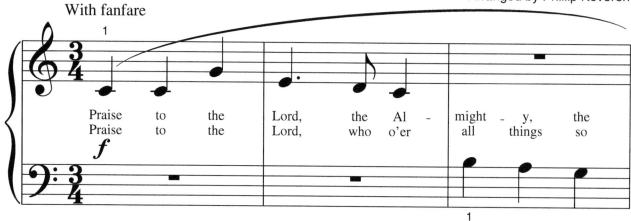

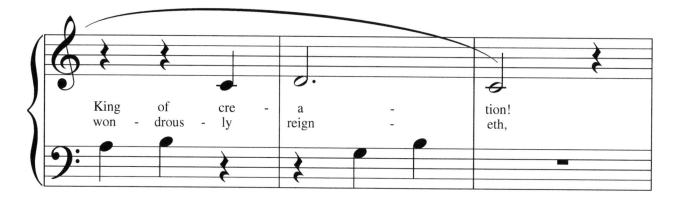

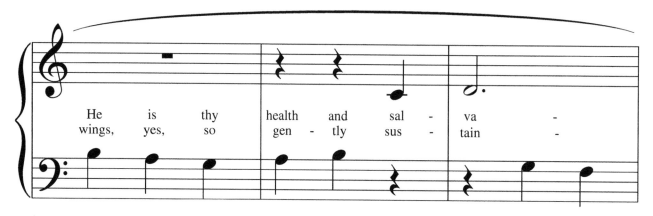

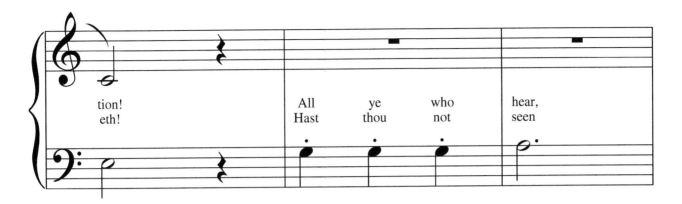

tion!   All   ye   who   hear,
eth!   Hast   thou   not   seen

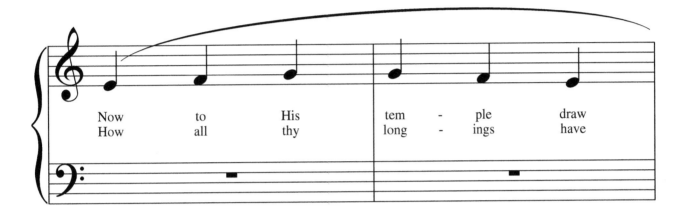

Now   to   His   tem – ple   draw
How   all   thy   long – ings   have

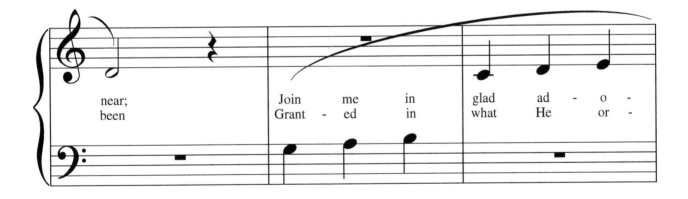

near;   Join   me   in   glad   ad – o –
been   Grant – ed   in   what   He   or –

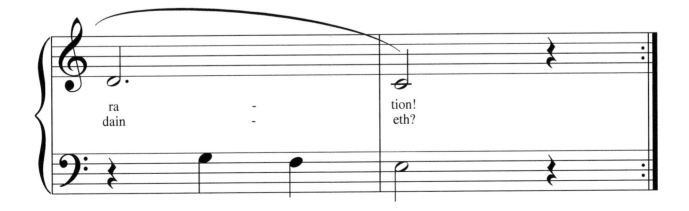

ra   –   tion!
dain   –   eth?

REJOICE, THE LORD IS KING

Words by CHARLES WESLEY
Music by JOHN DARWALL
Arranged by Phillip Keveren

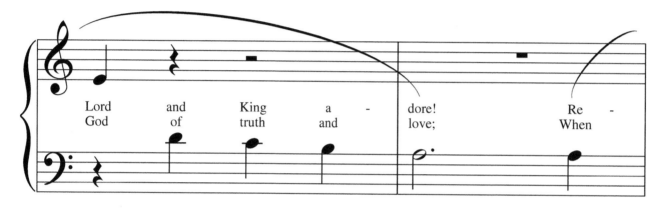

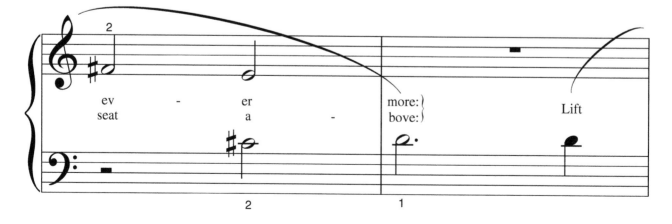

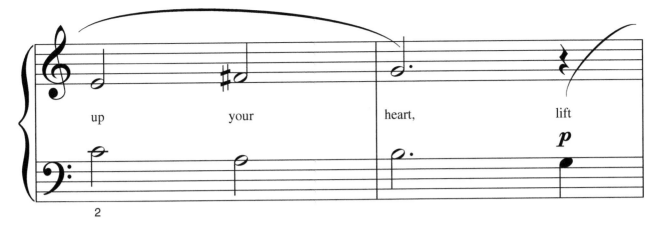

up   your   heart,   lift

p

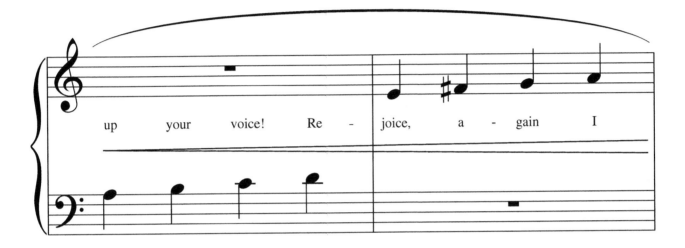

up   your   voice!   Re - joice,   a - gain   I

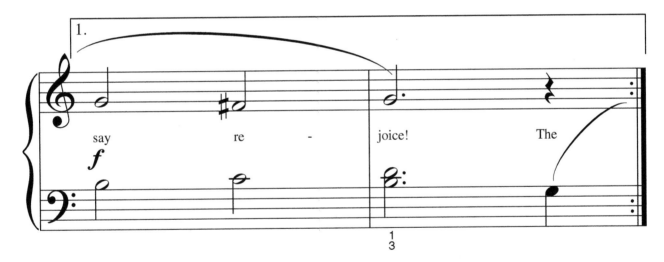

1.

say   re - joice!   The

f

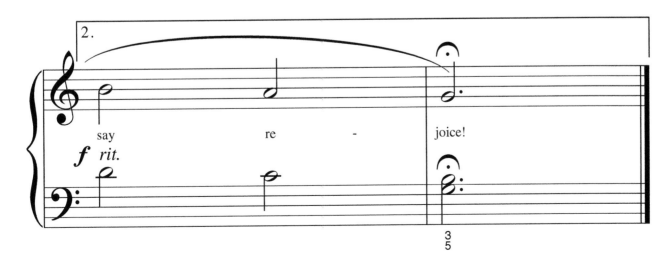

2.

say   re - joice!

f rit.

ROCK OF AGES

Words by AUGUSTUS M. TOPLADY
Music by THOMAS HASTINGS
Arranged by Phillip Keveren

Slowly, lilting

Rock of A - ges, cleft for me, Let me

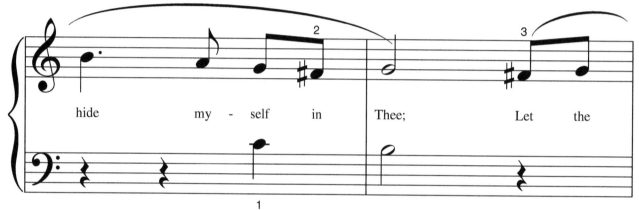

hide my - self in Thee; Let the

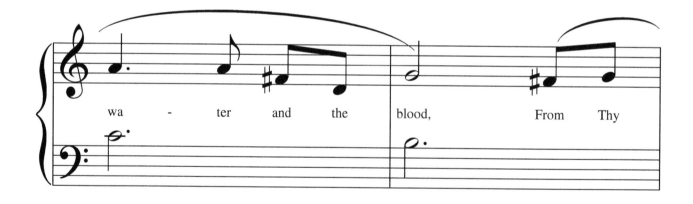

wa - ter and the blood, From Thy

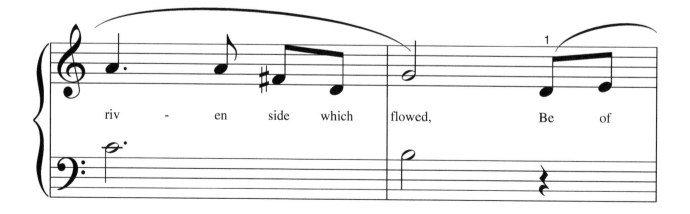

riv - en side which flowed, Be of

sin   the   dou - ble   cure,   Cleanse me

from   its   guilt   and   pow'r.   Not   the

mf

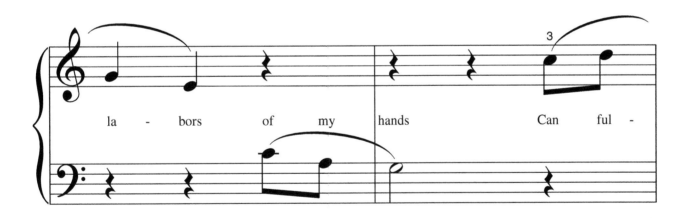

la - bors   of   my   hands   Can   ful -

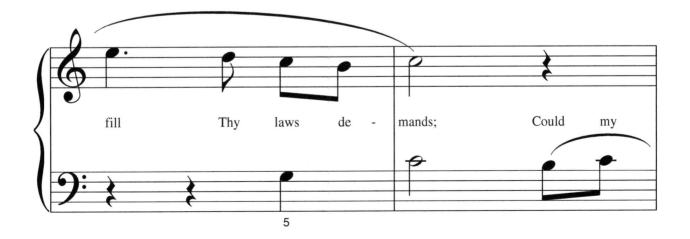

fill   Thy   laws   de - mands;   Could   my

5

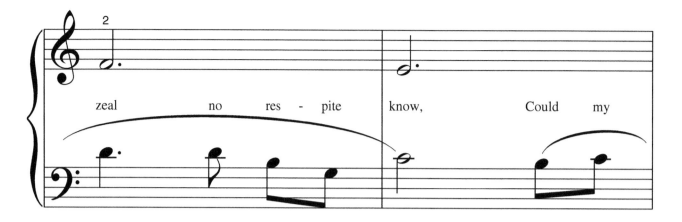

zeal no res - pite know, Could my

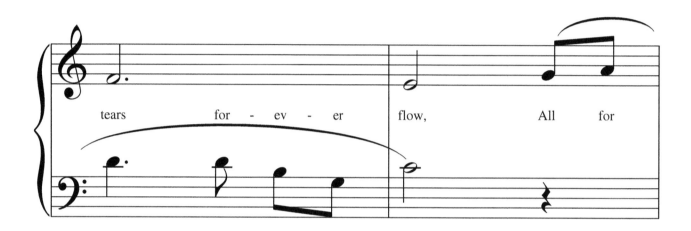

tears for - ev - er flow, All for

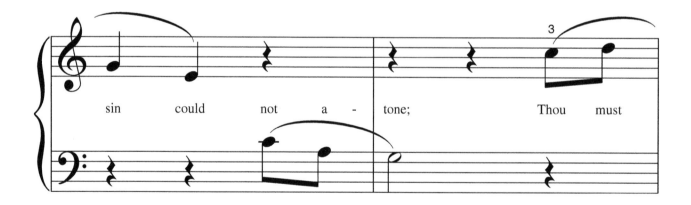

sin could not a - tone; Thou must

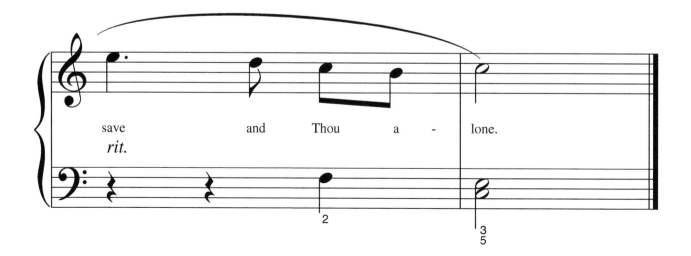

save and Thou a - lone.

rit.

SOFTLY AND TENDERLY

Words and Music by WILL L. THOMPSON
Arranged by Phillip Keveren

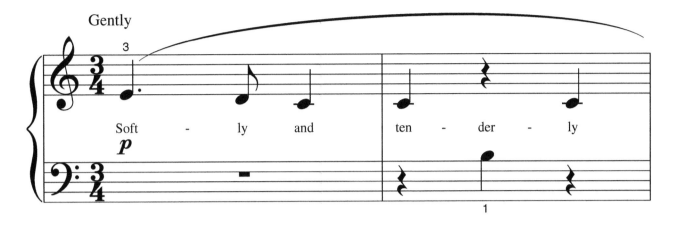

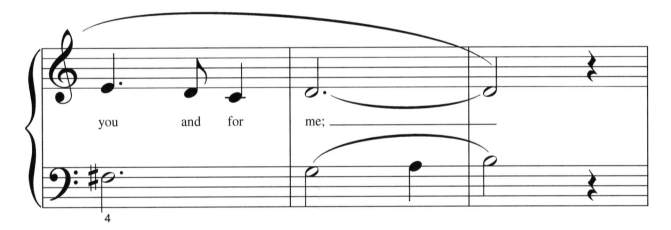

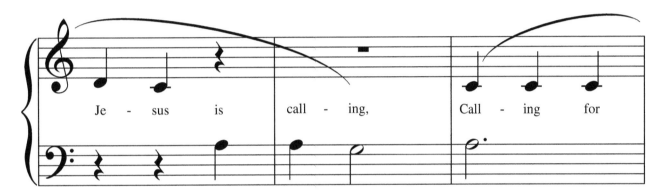

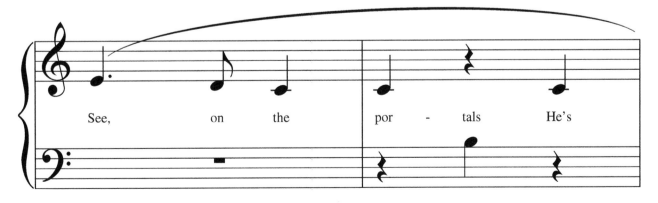

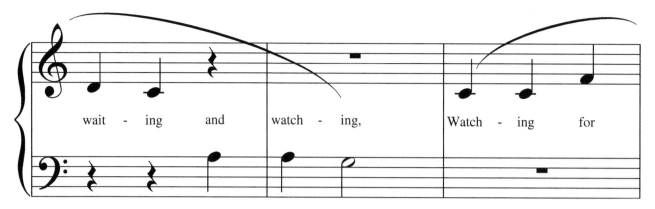

wait - ing and watch - ing, Watch - ing for

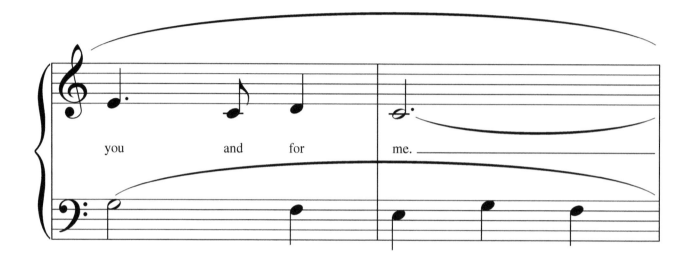

you and for me.

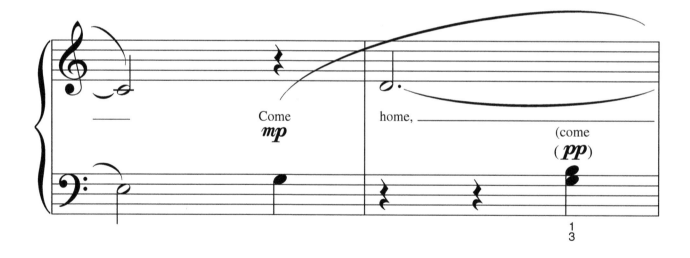

Come home,
mp
(come
(pp)

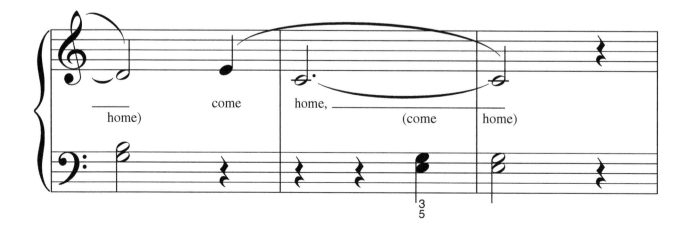

home) come home,
(come home)

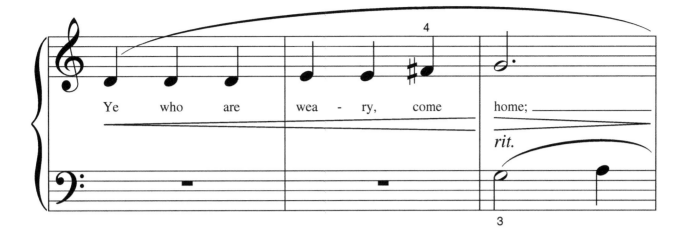

Ye who are wea - ry, come home; *rit.*

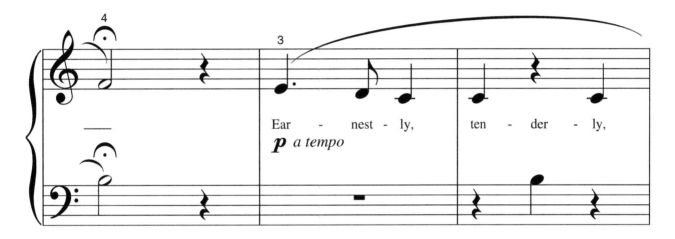

Ear - nest - ly, ten - der - ly,
p *a tempo*

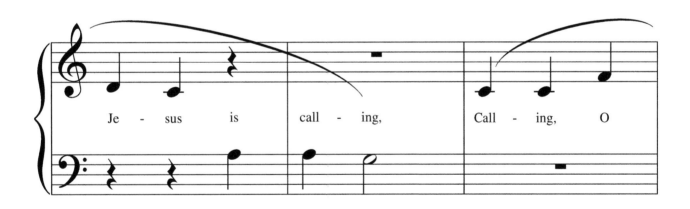

Je - sus is call - ing, Call - ing, O

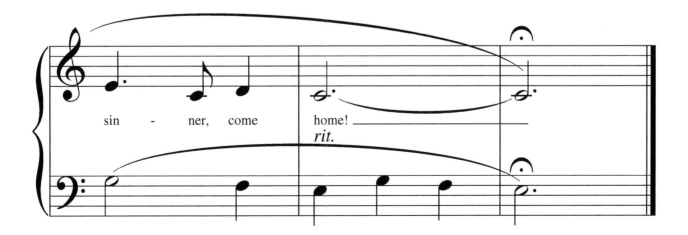

sin - ner, come home! *rit.*

A SHELTER IN THE TIME OF STORM

Words and Music by IRA D. SANKEY
Adapted by VERNON J. CHARLESWORTH
Arranged by Phillip Keveren

Steadily

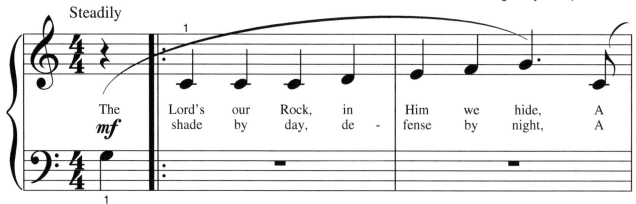

The
Lord's our Rock, in Him we hide, A
shade by day, de - fense by night, A

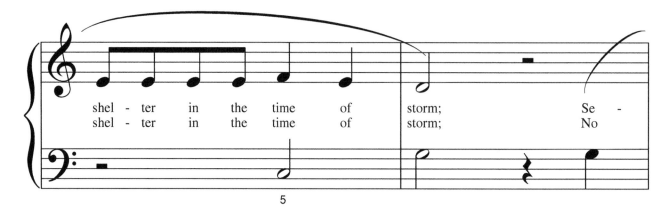

shel - ter in the time of storm; Se -
shel - ter in the time of storm; No

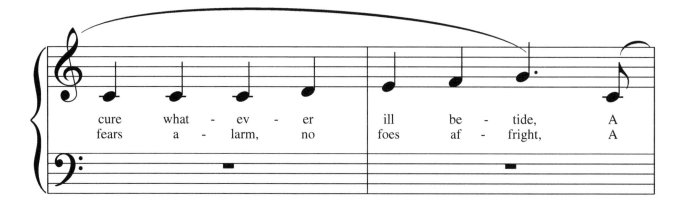

cure what - ev - er ill be - tide, A
fears a - larm, no foes af - fright, A

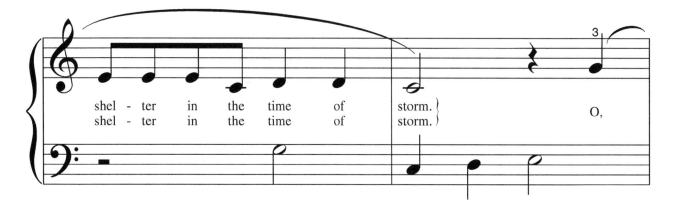

shel - ter in the time of storm.
shel - ter in the time of storm.
O,

Je - sus is a Rock in a wea - ry land, A

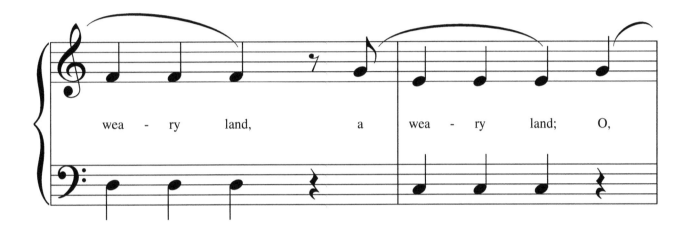

wea - ry land, a wea - ry land; O,

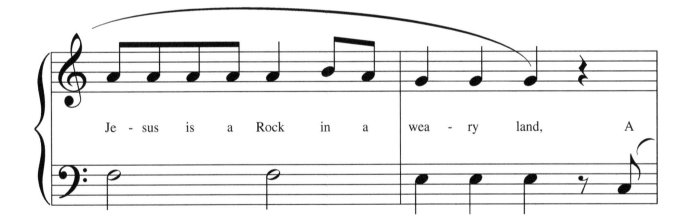

Je - sus is a Rock in a wea - ry land, A

shel - ter in the time of storm. A storm.

STAND UP, STAND UP FOR JESUS

Words by GEORGE DUFFIELD, JR.
Music by GEORGE J. WEBB
Arranged by Phillip Keveren

Victoriously

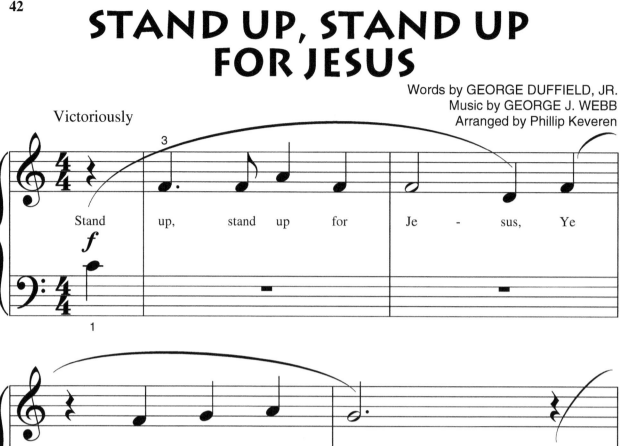

Stand up, stand up for Je - sus, Ye

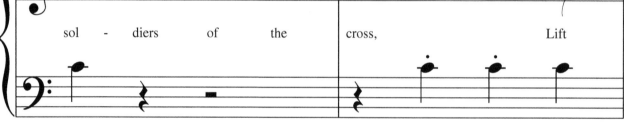

sol - diers of the cross, Lift

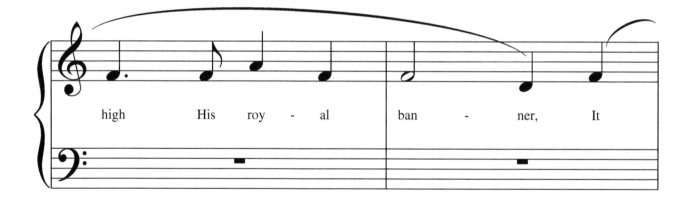

high His roy - al ban - ner, It

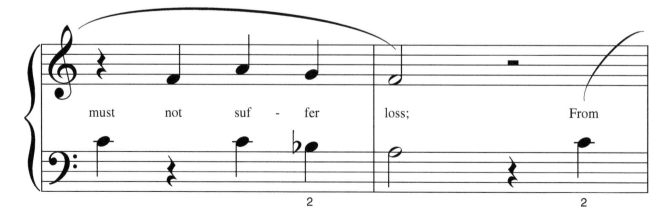

must not suf - fer loss; From

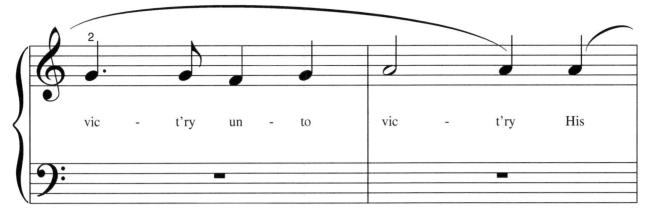

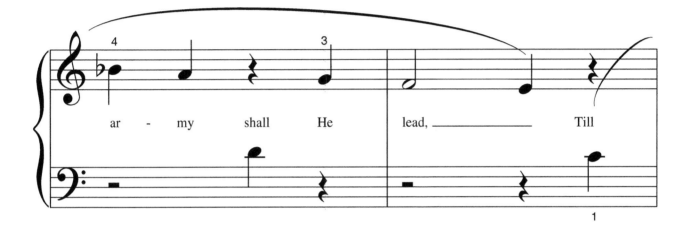

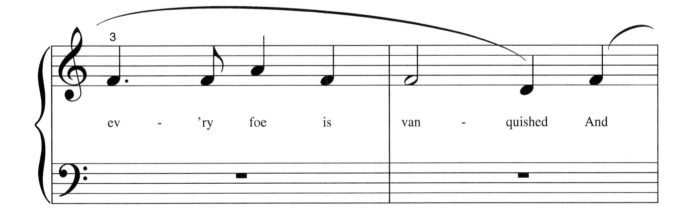

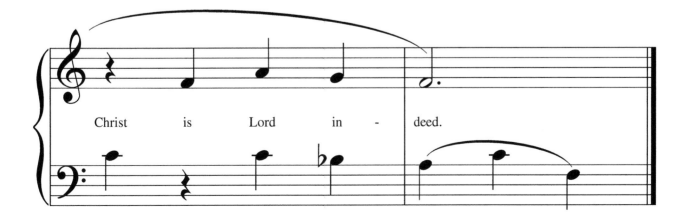

'TIS SO SWEET TO TRUST IN JESUS

Words by LOUISA M.R. STEAD
Music by WILLIAM J. KIRKPATRICK
Arranged by Phillip Keveren

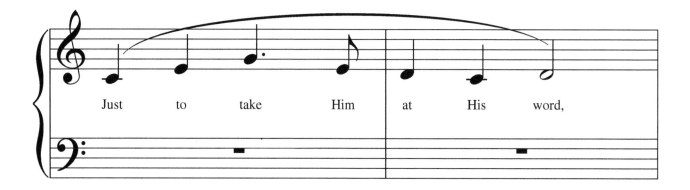

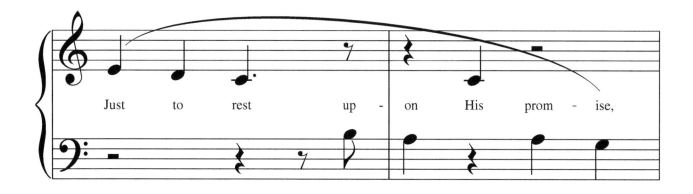

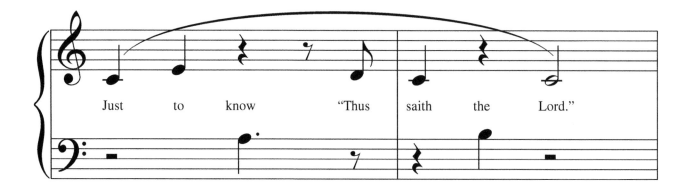

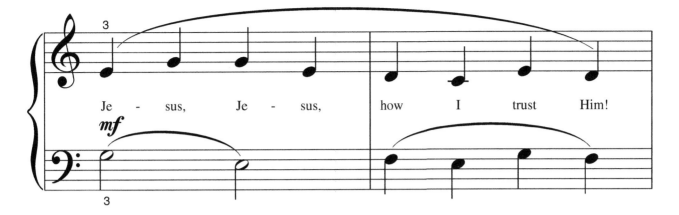

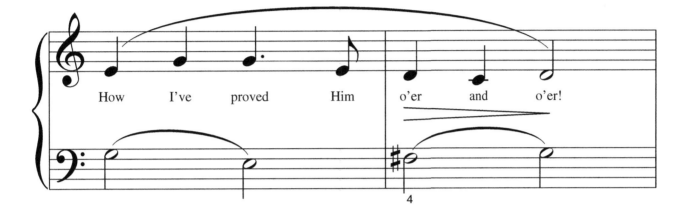

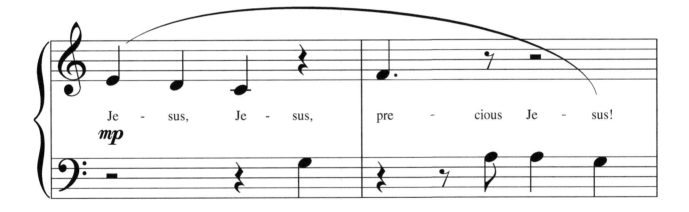

TRUST AND OBEY

Words by JOHN H. SAMMIS
Music by DANIEL B. TOWNER
Arranged by Philip Keveren

Peacefully

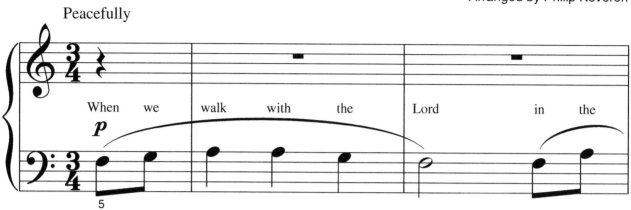

When we walk with the Lord in the

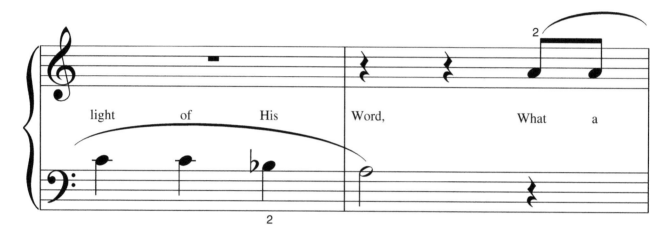

light of His Word, What a

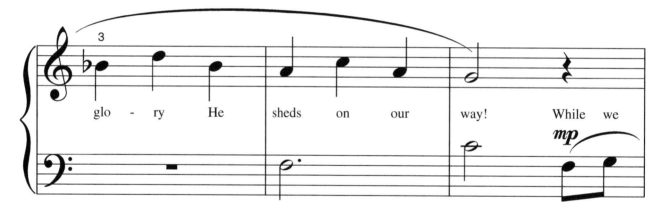

glo - ry He sheds on our way! While we

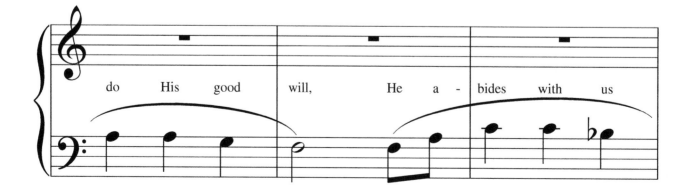

do His good will, He a - bides with us

still, And with all who will trust and o-

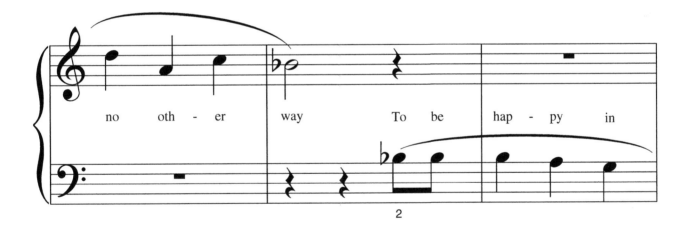

bey. Trust and o - bey, for there's

mf

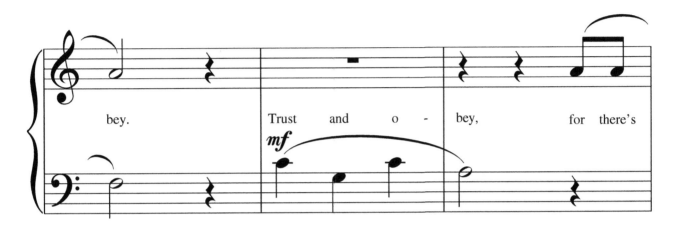

no oth - er way To be hap - py in

Je - sus, But to trust and o - bey.

rit.

THE PHILLIP KEVEREN SERIES

PIANO SOLO

EASY PIANO

BIG-NOTE PIANO

BEGINNING PIANO SOLOS

PIANO DUET

Prices, contents, and availability subject to change without notice.